A LEGACY *of* HOPE

60 YEARS OF LAKEWOOD CHURCH

Preface

Lakewood Church, whether meeting in a small feed store or the former Compaq Center, has always had the same mission—to share the love and hope of Christ with all people. Pastors John and Dodie Osteen held the first service on Mother's Day in 1959 with 90 faithful people and a passion to impact the community, the city of Houston, and the nations of the world. Over the next 40 years, this is exactly what they did.

When Pastor John went home to be with the Lord in 1999, although the congregation was grieving the loss of their beloved pastor, Joel was celebrated as he stepped into his father's shoes as the Senior Pastor of Lakewood Church. God continues to do exceedingly and abundantly above all that we could ask or think under the leadership of our pastors, Joel and Victoria Osteen.

This book was written to celebrate the history of the faithful people who have defined the heart of Lakewood for the last 60 years and to remember the miracles that God has done for us as a church. Whatever part you have played in Lakewood's history—thank you. Thank you for your love, your support, and your service. We couldn't have done it without you! We are excited to partner with you for the next 60 years as we believe that our best days are still out in front of us. We are believing for the exceeding, abundant, above and beyond as we carry the message of hope to Houston and the world.

"Behold, I stand at the door and knock. If anyone hears My voice and opens the door, I will come in to him and eat with him, and he with Me."

REVELATION 3:20

CHAPTER I

The Founders

Pastors John and Dodie Osteen

John Hillery Osteen

—

John Hillery Osteen was born to Ella Mae and Willis Jackson Osteen on August 21, 1921, in the small town of Paris, Texas. He and his five siblings began working as young children on their cotton farm to help support their family. After losing their farm during the Great Depression, the Osteen family relocated to Ft. Worth, Texas. As a teen, John dropped out of high school and began working at the Isis Theater. He would soon make a decision that would forever alter the course of his life and the generations that would come after him.

As a seventeen-year-old, John was wandering home from a nightclub at two o'clock in the morning when he began to consider the purpose of his life. He looked up at the stars and knew in

that moment that there was a God, and perhaps this God was the solution to his purposelessness.

Upon returning home, John opened the large, dusty family Bible. He was met with the picture of Jesus knocking on a door. It was a picture of Revelation 3:20, which reads, *"Behold, I stand at the door and knock. If anyone hears My voice and opens the door,*

Isis Theater, Ft. Worth, Texas

Sam Martin

John Osteen

John Osteen and his friend
Sam Martin;
Central Baptist Church,
Baytown, Texas

I will come in to him and eat with him, and he with Me." The next day, John committed his life to Christ at Grace Church in Ft. Worth, Texas, led by his friend Sam Martin, who had been telling him about Jesus' love in high school.

John Osteen began to preach on street corners, at nursing homes, Bible studies, youth groups, and anywhere else that would welcome him.

John saw no reason to wait to tell people about the love that he had received in Christ. He went back to high school and eventually decided to pursue a bachelor's degree in Theology to be better equipped to teach the Word. John graduated with his bachelor's in Theology from John Brown University in Siloam Springs, Arkansas. Two years later, John graduated with a master's degree from Northern Theological Seminary in Chicago, Illinois. He took temporary pastoral positions in San Francisco, California, and Hamlin, Texas. Eventually, he settled in Baytown, Texas, in the late 1940s, where he met his wife, Dodie Pilgrim, a nurse at a local hospital who was also a member of his church.

Certificate of Ordination of Pastor John Osteen, 1942

STATE OF ARKANSAS
COUNTY OF BENTON } SS.

I,.., the duly elected, commissioned, qualified and acting Clerk of the County and Probate Courts in and for the County and State aforesaid, do hereby certify that the instrument annexed hereto is a true, perfect and complete copy of

Certificate of Ordination of John H. Osteen

as the same appears of record in..............Minister's Credentials Record "1"..............at page.......151...... thereof; said record being on file in my said office.

In testimony whereof, I have hereunto set my hand and official seal this 4th day of........August............, 194 2

E. F. Buttram

County and Probate Clerk, Benton County, Arkansas.

John Osteen as a baby

John Osteen with his parents

As a teenager

August 21, 1921:
Born in Paris, Texas, to Lee Ella Mae and Willis Jackson Osteen

1938:
At the age of 17, John Osteen gave his life to the Lord

1938-1939:
1st year of preaching

1938:
Graduated from high school in Ft. Worth, Texas

1942:
Graduated from John Brown University in Siloam Springs, Arkansas

John (right) and brother Jack

John and Dodie Osteen

1944:
‣ Graduated from Northern Theological Seminary in Chicago, Illinois
‣ Pastored in San Francisco, California
‣ Pastored at First Baptist in Hamlin, Texas

Late 1940s:
Pastored at Central Baptist Church in Baytown, Texas, where he met Dolores (Dodie) Pilgrim

September 17, 1954:
Married Dodie Pilgrim

1957-1959:
Pastored at Hibbard Memorial Church in Houston, Texas

Dodie Osteen as a nursing student

Dolores (Dodie) Ann Pilgrim

—

Dolores (Dodie) Ann Pilgrim was born on October 22, 1933, in what was known at the time as Pelly, Texas. Since this time, the town has been renamed Baytown. The only child of Georgia Lee and Roy Vernon Pilgrim, Dodie grew up with great attention and affection from her parents. When she was 18 months old, Dodie was diagnosed with polio and required special care for a time. However, she was miraculously not confined to a wheelchair and only wore leg braces until the fourth grade.

At the age of 12, Dodie gave her life to the Lord. Eight years later, she graduated from Lillie Jolly School of Nursing in Houston, Texas, with her degree in nursing. Only days after passing the state board nursing exam, she married the love of her life, John Osteen, on September 17, 1954.

Dodie as a teen; Dodie and her father; Dodie's childhood home; Georgia Lee and Roy Vernon Pilgrim

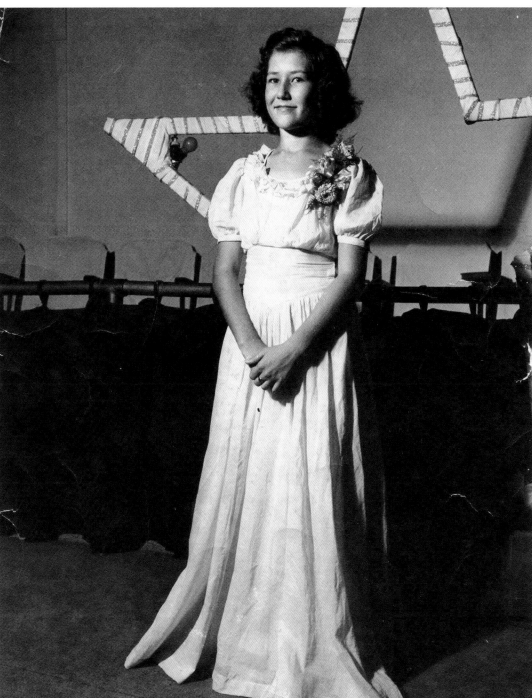

As a baby

Age 2

Age 5

October 22, 1933:
Born in Pelly, Texas (renamed Baytown in 1948), to Georgia Lee and Roy Pilgrim and would be their only child

At 18 months, Dodie was diagnosed with polio, but was miraculously not bound to a wheelchair and only wore a brace until the fourth grade

1945:
At the age of 12, Dodie gave her life to the Lord

Age 7   Age 12   In high school band

1951:   **August 1954:**   **September 9-10, 1954:**   **September 17, 1954:**
Graduated from Robert E. Lee High School   Graduated from Lillie Jolly School of Nursing   State Board Exams   Married John Hillery Osteen
                                             (affiliated with Memorial Hospital)

September 17, 1954
John and Dodie Osteen's wedding

Wedding shower

PAUL KENT OSTEEN

LISA KELLEY OSTEEN

The Osteen Family

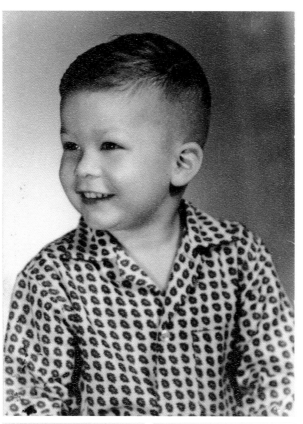

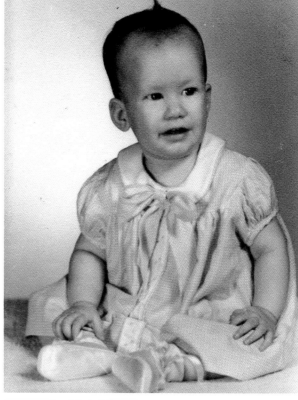

TAMARA ANN OSTEEN

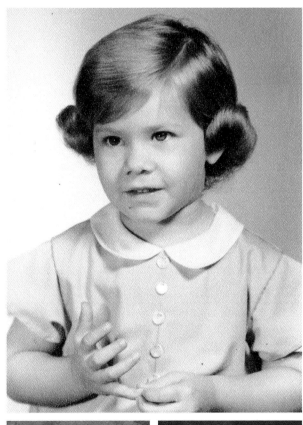

JOEL SCOTT OSTEEN

APRIL LEIGH OSTEEN

"It started out with John loving people. He didn't care whether they were rich or poor, young or old, he would love them."

DODIE OSTEEN

CHAPTER II

The Beginning

The First 10 Years

Pastor John arriving at the India Airport in 1968;
The original revival tent in 1959

Pastor John Osteen appeared on television several times in the 60s

The Beginning
The First 10 Years

—

In 1958, Pastor John was pastoring at Hibbard Memorial Baptist Church in Houston, Texas, when his first daughter, Lisa, was born with a crippling disease similar to cerebral palsy. Pastor John sought God in the midst of this personal crisis and started to wonder if the healing he read about in the Bible was possible today. He and Dodie decided to believe for the impossible. They stood on the Word of God and believed that as Jesus healed in the past, He could do the same for them since Hebrews 13:8 says that Jesus is the same yesterday, today, and forever.

John and Dodie decided to believe for the impossible.

Before she was one year old, Lisa was completely healed and Pastor John was ignited with a message of faith. Unfortunately, the church he was a part of was not receptive of his new message. Although he

Pastor John Osteen received the baptism of the Holy Spirit and began to preach about a God who would heal the sick, perform miracles, and baptize all believers in the power of the Holy Spirit.

was permitted to remain as pastor by the church board after being put on trial for heresy, Pastor John decided to step down from his position and start his own church.

Lakewood Baptist Church first met at Smiley High School on Mother's Day 1959 with 90 members on foldout chairs in northeast Houston, then in a tent on a shopping center's lot until they purchased a small, abandoned feed store, which became their sanctuary.

Such Peace

Marilyn Morrison

It was in 1963 that a friend invited me to come to church with her. So I just said, "Okay." I went to church and I'll never forget the first time I walked in that feed store. Brother Osteen was there. He was preaching and I thought, "What is this? Such peace and everybody's happy. Where am I at?" And I loved it.

1990s' recreation of the feed store church

The Feed Store

Dodie Osteen

John had been praying about a building, but we didn't have any money to start a church or anything. Mrs. Lawson said, "I have a feed store down here. You can use it."

I remember the first time I went into the feed store. It was just an old barnlike building with slits in the floor so that the hay could fall through. It had no restroom. I don't think it had a drinking fountain or anything. It was pretty pitiful, pretty slim pickings, but we worked on it. We eventually built a restroom separate from the church and purchased the building for not very much.

It was no beautiful building to look at. It had nothing pretty in it, but the people loved it. They just loved being there.

The First 90

Dodie Osteen

The first 90 people came because they heard about John; some from the church we had just left, and others from the neighborhood. Sonny and Ruth Lindsey, Bill and Ruthie Dearman, Curtis and Ann Bell and R. W. and Angela Smith were some of the people that came. Bill and Curtis were elders, and I remember Bertha Nichols led the singing. They were all so wonderful. They treated John and me so well. I'm telling you, they loved us. They would've fought for us, and we would've done the same for them.

1959 Revival at Lakewood Baptist Church

1958
▸ Pastor John Osteen received the baptism of the Holy Spirit and began to preach about a God who would heal the sick, perform miracles, and baptize all believers in the power of the Holy Spirit.

1959
▸ After being put on trial for heresy, but ultimately allowed to stay as pastor, Pastor John Osteen left the Hibbard Memorial Church to start his own church.
▸ **May 10:** Pastors John and Dodie Osteen opened Lakewood Baptist Church on Mother's Day with 90 members and held services in Smiley High School.
▸ A few weeks after opening the church, the Full Gospel Business Men's Fellowship loaned Lakewood Baptist Church a tent so they could hold their weekly services at the shopping center on Mesa Road.
▸ **September:** The church moved into their new home, the abandoned feed store.

1961
▸ **February:** Pastor John Osteen resigned as pastor of Lakewood Baptist Church to begin 8 years of evangelizing all over the world.
▸ **March:** Marvin Crow became pastor of Lakewood Baptist Church.
▸ **September:** Hurricane Carla blew down the word "Baptist" on the church's sign and the church was renamed "Lakewood Church."

1969
▸ Pastor John Osteen returned to Houston to pastor Lakewood Church with a vision to reach the world with the Gospel.
▸ Lakewood Church began hosting an annual Thanksgiving Convention and Ministers Conference.

Early Missions

Dodie Osteen

After starting Lakewood, John was only there a short period of time. We started the church in '59 and he stayed there until '61. Then he felt the call to go all over the world. He had reaching the lost on his heart. He always told the congregation, "We must reach the unreached and tell the untold." He chose a young man named Marvin Crow to take over the church, and John preached in the Philippines, India and Mexico. After eight years, God spoke to John to come back home and pastor the church.

Pastor John Osteen in the Philippine Islands

Pastor John Osteen held crusades all over the world

Two years after starting Lakewood Baptist Church, Pastor John resigned as pastor, feeling a call to missionary efforts. He chose a young man named Marvin Crow to take over the church, and Pastor John Osteen preached in the Philippines, India and Mexico. Eight years later, after evangelizing all over the world, Pastor John returned to his role as pastor of Lakewood Church with a renewed passion for reaching the world with the Gospel. This same year, pastors from all over Houston gathered at Lakewood's first annual Leadership Conference.

"Faith Conquest," an early publication from Pastor John Osteen

FAITH CONQUEST

DECEMBER 1961

International Voice of The Osteen Evangelistic Ministry

IN THIS ISSUE:

Holy Ghost Outpouring in Houston, Texas, Southern Baptist Church

"PENTECOST IS NOT A DENOMINATION BUT AN EXPERIENCE FROM GOD FOR EVERYONE"

Rev. John H. Osteen, former Pastor of this Great Central Baptist Church, Baytown, Texas

Wonders and Miracles Come to Houston

Mrs. Ernest Duncan, on left, was afflicted in her vocal cords. She could not speak above a whisper. God healed her instantly. As a result of seeing this miracle, two Baptist preachers who were present, received the Baptism of the Holy Ghost.

Mrs. E. E. Fergeson, on right, wife of Chairman of Board of Deacons, was one of the first members to receive the Baptism of the Holy Ghost. She and her husband started this religious bookstore as a result of God moving in their lives.

MARY CLAYTON

The first miracle we at this Southern Baptist Church witnessed was performed on this young lady's body. She was crippled in the ankle and foot. Her ankle was stiff as steel. It popped like a gun and became normal instantly. She discarded her specially built-up shoe and has been normal ever since. Since receiving Baptism of the Holy Ghost she frequently speaks Spanish though she knows not a word of Spanish.

Mrs. I. B. Buckles of Houston. Healed of serious blood and heart disease. When her test revealed the fact that she was healed she told the Doctor about Brother Osteen praying for her. He said he rejoiced with her and encouraged her to continue to have faith in God.

PAUL and LISA OSTEEN

These are two of Bro. and Mrs. Osteen's children. Paul had eight warts disappear from his body after his mother prayed for him.

Lisa was abnormal at birth. God healed her by a miracle. She is perfectly normal.

7

"Well, you could say, every church thinks they're special, and they have a place, and so on. Everybody should think that about their own church. But I got this distinctive feeling or thought during the process, and not in an arrogant way, that we had a special place, a special purpose. The missions was a big component of that, the missions to the world, missions to the city. There was a special purpose for Lakewood."

CARL SMITH, *original member*

CHAPTER III

The Expansion Decade

The 70s

Pastors John and Dodie Osteen speaking at Lakewood

The Expansion Decade
The 70s

—

After the congregation of 90 had been together for nearly a decade, word about Pastor John's powerful message of faith began to spread throughout Houston. The overwhelming theme from its congregants was that they felt so loved. Thus, Lakewood later became affectionately known as "The Oasis of Love."

Pastors John and Dodie Osteen at the construction site

Construction site; Renee Branson; Curtis Bell, Pastor John Osteen, Bill Dearman; Joel Osteen

In 1973, Lakewood Church built its new 700-seat sanctuary with the help of Curtis Bell. Only two years later, Lakewood had to expand to seat 1,800, and two years after that to seat 4,000. People were recognizing that God was moving and they attended from all over the Houston area. In 1979, Lakewood expanded to seat 5,000 people. Along with weekly services, small groups, and Bible studies, Lakewood began its annual Thanksgiving Conference where ministers and missionaries from all over the world came to be encouraged and equipped.

The construction of Lakewood Church

1973
As the number of church members began to rise, Lakewood Church built a new 700-seat sanctuary with the help, planning, and directing of Curtis Bell.

1975
Expanded to seat 1800 people

1977
Expanded to seat 4000 people

1979
▸ Expanded to seat 5000 people
▸ Begins hosting an annual Thanksgiving Convention and Ministries Conference with thousands in attendance.

The feed store building was remodeled and became the church offices

The Three Things

Dodie Osteen

After John came back from preaching all over the world, God impressed upon him to emphasize three things: worship God, preach God's Word, and reach the world with the Gospel. He started doing that, and I'm telling you, people started coming from everywhere in the city, and the church just kept growing. John always made sure that there was always a map in the sanctuary to represent the nations of the world. Eventually, the map turned into a display of flags, and then the globe that we see today.

A Big Family

Dan Kelly

It was wonderful. It was like a big, big family. We'd come into the service in the morning and stay there all day. We'd all go together, eat someplace, and come back to the night service. So you leave in the morning, and you wouldn't come back until the third service was over. Everybody knew everybody. It was just a wonderful place. It would lift you up. If you were a stranger off the street and you were going through something difficult, as soon as you stepped in the door, you knew it. It lifted you up.

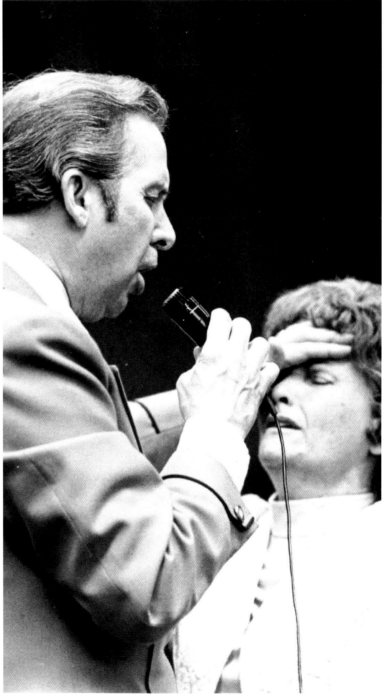

Expect a Miracle

Dawn Smith

The main thing that I remember, when I first started coming, was there was a lightness like I've never felt before. I remember looking at the podium and there was a little sign on the podium that said, "Expect a Miracle." Every time I came to church, I saw "Expect a Miracle." There was such an expectation when you came to the church that God was there and He's going to do something for you or He's going to bless you. You always had expectation when you walked through the doors.

My parents didn't want me to leave their church, but they only had church on Sunday morning. So I came over to Lakewood on Sunday nights and Wednesday nights. I don't believe I missed a service, unless I was out of town or something. But I just couldn't wait to get there, every time. I remember walking in the doors, I mean, walking in, going, "Oh, I'm here again. I just love this place." There was something in the atmosphere, like nothing ... like nothing I had ever felt before.

Curtis Bell shaking hands with Kenneth and Oretha Hagin, Dodie Osteen

Thanksgiving Convention

Dodie Osteen

People from all nations would come to the annual Thanksgiving Convention and John had little cottages built in the back. Lisa and I would go out and decorate them, clean them up, and hang curtains. Can you imagine me doing all that? I used to do a lot of that, even hang wallpaper for other people. Anyway, we would fix up the cottages, and if any missionaries or ministers didn't have a place to stay, they would come stay there. We built a cafeteria and were able to feed the missionaries. You don't know how many people came, how many people from India, Africa, Mexico, the Philippines and other places. They loved it, and John was so good to them.

Dodie Osteen preaching

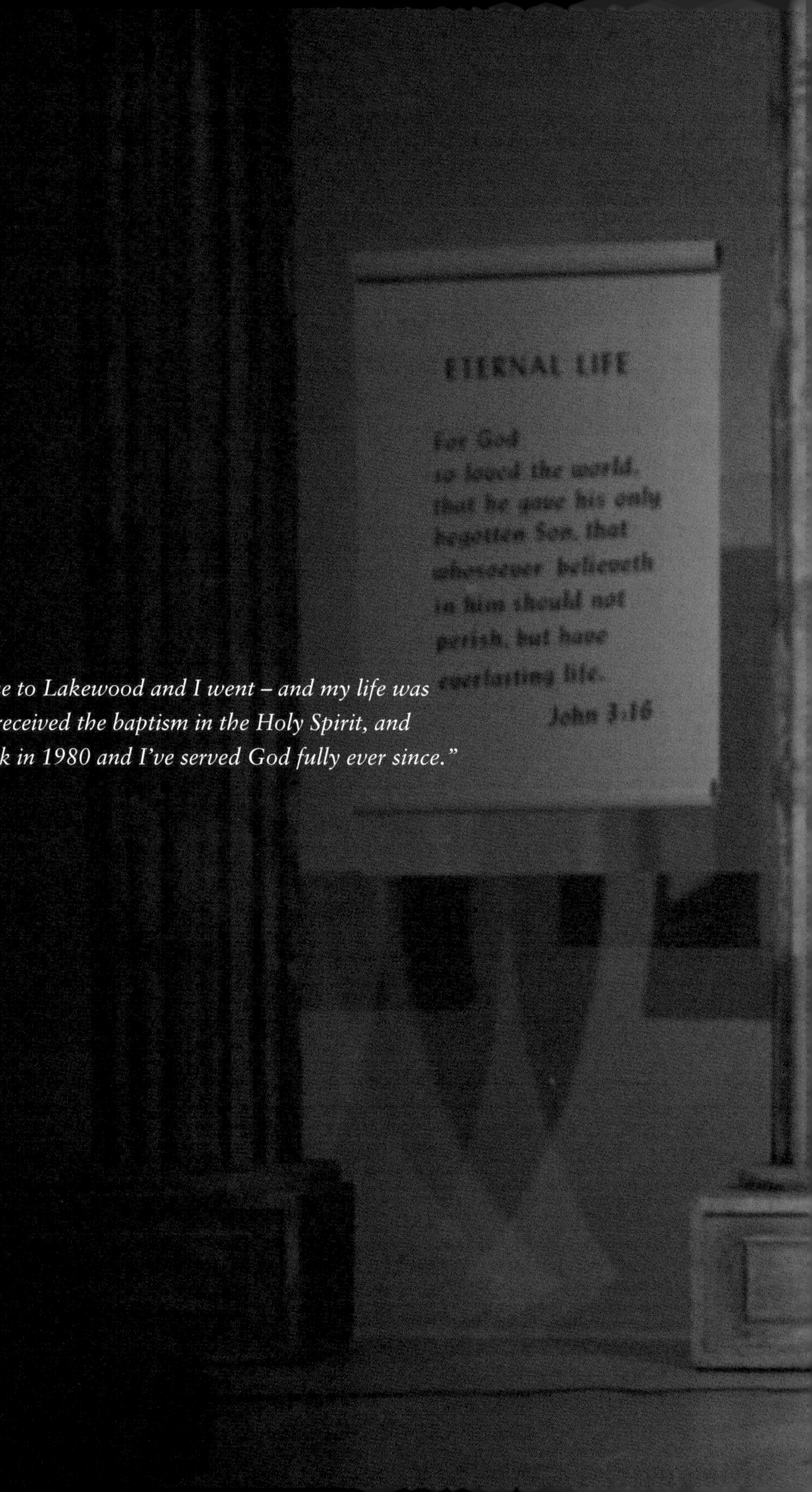

"When I was 20 and living in Houston, a roommate invited me to Lakewood and I went – and my life was forever changed! I totally committed myself to serving God, received the baptism in the Holy Spirit, and started on a mission to get all my family saved! That was back in 1980 and I've served God fully ever since."

SUSIE COLLINS

ETERNAL LIFE

For God
so loved the world,
that he gave his only
begotten Son, that
whosoever believeth
in him should not
perish, but have
everlasting life.

John 3:16

THE HOLY SPIRIT

If ye then, being evil
know how to give go
gifts unto your chil
how much mo
your heaven
the Holy S
that ask H

UNCHANGING SAVIOUR

Jesus Christ the same
yesterday, and today,
and forever.

Hebrews 13:8

CHAPTER IV

Miracles and TV Ministry

The 80s

Miracles and TV Ministry

—

In 1981, the Osteens' world came to a sudden halt in the midst of some of their greatest years of ministry, when Dodie was diagnosed with metastatic cancer of the liver and given only weeks to live with no treatment available. Pastor John, Dodie, and the rest of the family decided to believe for the miraculous and Dodie received her miracle. Following her healing, Dodie had a passion to see others receive healing as she had. She began praying for the sick in all church services and began a healing ministry that she continues today. Out of this experience, Dodie wrote a book with her testimony called *Healed of Cancer*, which continues to be a bestselling book. Pastor John was noted as one of the first pastors to call his wife a co-pastor and have her partner with him in pulpit ministry. After Pastor John broke the mold, many other pastors followed.

Pastor John, Dodie, and the rest of the family decided to believe for the miraculous, and Dodie received her miracle.

"I am going to take my wife home. We are going to pray and seek God, and then we will decide what to do. We believe in miracles, and we believe in the Miracle Worker."

Pastor John Osteen

Pastors John and Dodie Osteen, 1988

We Believe in Miracles

Dodie Osteen

In 1981, I hadn't been feeling well. I had begun to have some symptoms that were disturbing to me. So, I went into the hospital, but after 20 days of testing, I just wanted to go home. I never expected to get the diagnosis of cancer, and when I did, it was just unbelievable. It was a death sentence because they didn't have any treatment available at that time. They gave me a few weeks to live. I was devastated. The doctor had told John the diagnosis down in the lobby of the hospital, so he came to me. My husband came into the room and told me, and then all of the sudden I heard sobbing outside, and I said, "Who in the world is that crying?" It was my older son, Paul, who was in medical school, just sobbing because he knew what cancer of the liver could do to you. John told the doctor, "I am going to take my wife home. We are going to pray and seek God, and then we will decide what to do. We believe in miracles, and we believe in the Miracle Worker."

The day after I came home from the hospital, John and I prayed the prayer of agreement and put my case in the hands of the Lord. As far as I'm concerned, that day, December 11, 1981, my healing began. My body didn't feel healed. In fact, I felt terrible and I looked terrible. But I knew if I gave in to the way I felt, I wouldn't live. I felt like I was going to die so many times! But I fought and I stood firm, and I kept reminding God of His promises in His Word. And I was healed!

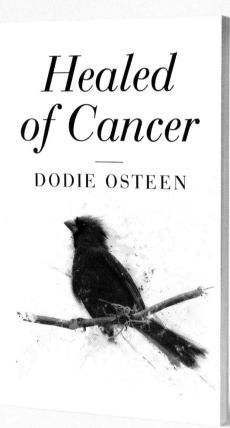

Dodie told her full story in her book *Healed of Cancer*, originally published in 1986

Joel helping in television ministry as a teen

Pastor John had a vision to reach the nations, and one of the ways that this could most effectively be done was through television ministry. The congregation of Lakewood stood behind Pastor John's vision for the television outreach, raising $1 million toward these efforts in only a year. Along with the new television ministry, Lakewood launched the World Satellite Network. This was the first Christian satellite network, allowing churches from all over the country to tune in to various Lakewood events.

In 1983, Joel came home from Oral Roberts University to help with starting the new television ministry. That same year, Lisa Osteen also returned home after graduating from Oral Roberts University to work at Lakewood full time, eventually becoming the Director of Volunteer Ministries.

Lisa also launched the Healing Center for Marriages that she led from 1983-1989. The Healing Center saw countless marriages restored and lives healed.

Lisa Osteen at the Healing Center for Marriages

Lakewood Church opened the Lakewood Bible Institute for those wanting to pursue greater education in ministry. Pastor John taught many of the classes along with an amazing faculty. During the few years that it was in session, it had over 100 graduates. During this time, Lakewood also launched its National Women's Convention that drew women from all across the world.

Tamara Osteen Graff and Jim Graff joined the Lakewood pastoral staff in 1986, where they faithfully served until 1988 when they moved to Victoria, Texas, to pastor Faith Family Church, which is still thriving today. On April 20, 1987, wedding bells rang as Joel Osteen and Victoria Iloff were married. Victoria would eventually resign from her job at her mother's jewelry store to volunteer at Lakewood and travel with Pastor John and Joel around the world. Justin Osteen, Pastor John's oldest son, joined the staff as administrator. April Osteen became the Lakewood youth pastor in 1988 and was later joined by her husband.

April 20, 1987
Joel and Victoria Osteen's wedding

Pastor John and Joel on the Amazon River in South America

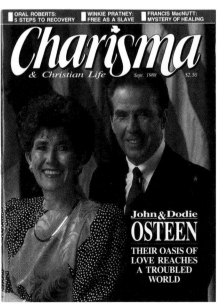

Charisma & Christian Life magazine

1981
▸ **December:** Dodie Osteen was diagnosed with metastatic cancer of the liver and given a few weeks to live, but was miraculously healed.
▸ Dodie's miraculous healing launched her into her prayer and healing ministry.
▸ Pastor John Osteen was noted as one of the first pastors to call his wife a co-pastor and have her do pulpit ministry. This gesture would soon be followed by hundreds of other pastors.

1982
▸ The congregation of Lakewood Church pledged $1 million to launch Lakewood's new television outreach ministry.

1983
▸ Lakewood Church began hosting the National Ladies Convention.
▸ Joel Osteen left Oral Roberts University to return home and aid in the beginning of the weekly "John Osteen" television program.
▸ Lisa Osteen returned home after graduating from Oral Roberts University to work full time at Lakewood Church. She would eventually become Director of Volunteer Ministries.
▸ Lakewood Church began Lakewood Bible Institute and had over 100 graduates in the years it was in operation.

1986
Dodie Osteen published her first book, *Healed of Cancer.*

1988
▸ Lakewood Church opened the new 8200-seat sanctuary on the northeast side of Houston.

Lakewood Church Groundbreaking, 1987

The Oasis of Love

Dodie Osteen

I think Bill Dearman came up with the phrase "The Oasis of Love." People would follow the bumper stickers to church. That's what was so amazing. Some of them got saved from following that bumper sticker to the church, became prayer partners and everything.

Family Life Center and Administrative Offices, 1993; Finished Lakewood Church; Sanctuary

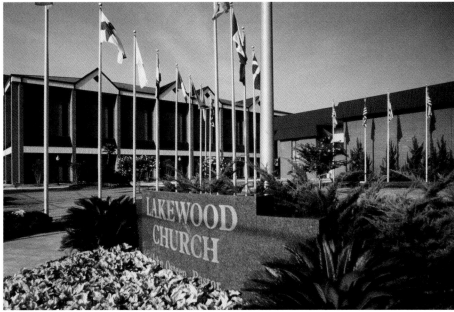

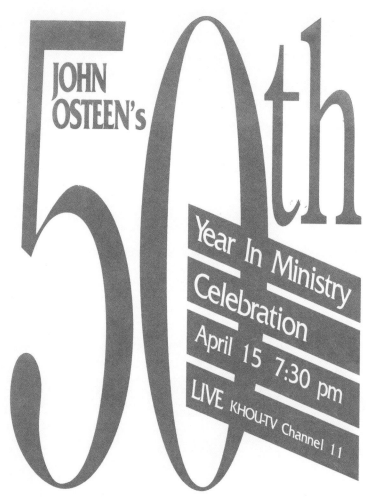

JOHN OSTEEN's **50th**

Year In Ministry Celebration

April 15 7:30 pm

LIVE KHOU-TV Channel 11

At the new "Oasis of Love"
7400 E. Houston Road
Houston, Texas 77028

Thanksgiving & Leadership Conference, 1981

November 25-29
at Lakewood Church

Cassette Teachings By:
- Charles Capps
- Norvel Hayes
- Marilyn Hickey
- T.L. Osborn
- John Osteen

THANKSGIVING CONVENTION

& LEADERSHIP CONFERENCE

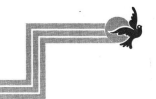

November 24-28, 1982
at Lakewood Church
Houston, Texas

Featuring Cassette Teaching By:

—Leslie Hale   —Norvel Hayes

—Daisy Osborn   —T. L. Osborn

—John Osteen   —R. W. Schambach

—Lester Sumrall

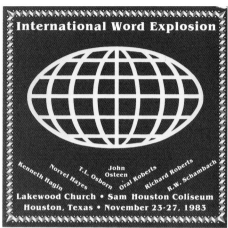

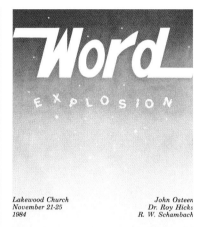

Gathering Believers from around the World

Lakewood hosted the most prominent ministers of the 80s to reach Houston and the world.

John Osteen's 50th Year in Ministry Celebration
1981—Thanksgiving & Leadership Conference
1982—Thanksgiving Convention & Leadership Conference
1983—Lakewood Ladies Convention
1983—Houston Word Explosion
1983—International Word Explosion

1984—Word Explosion
1985—3rd Annual Lakewood International Ladies Convention
1986—Word Explosion
1987—5th Lakewood International Ladies Convention
1988—18th Annual World Conference

NORTH AMERICA
Mexico

A Legacy of Missions

PASTOR JOHN OSTEEN'S MISSIONARY JOURNEYS

—

Pastor John traveled all over the world preaching, encouraging, and supporting pastors and ministries. His main focus was India, having traveled there over 40 times.

SOUTH AMERICA
Ecuador
Colombia
Venezuela

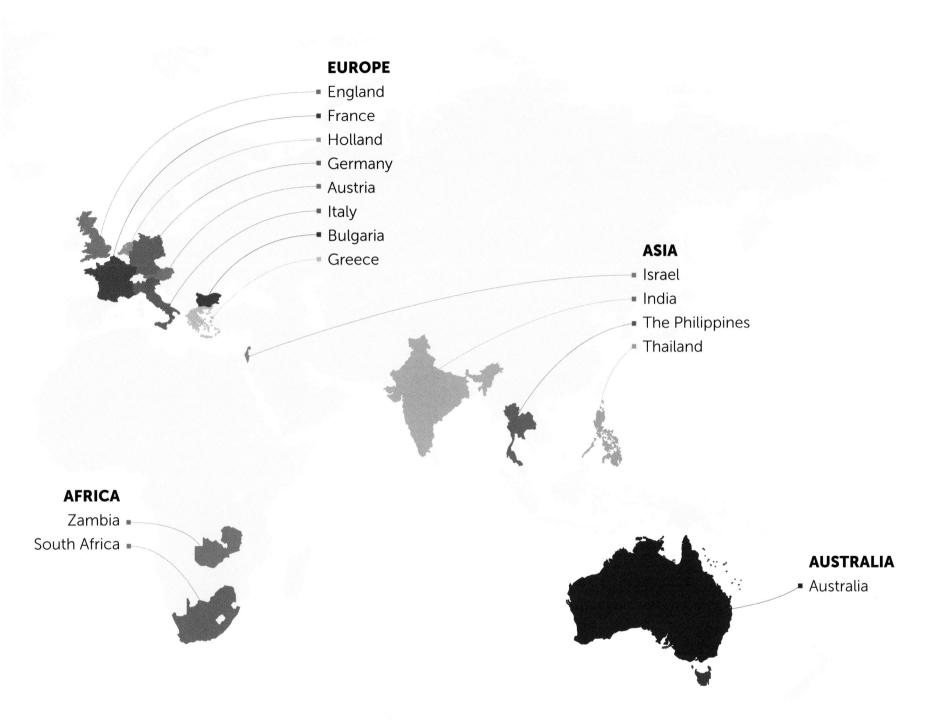

EUROPE
- England
- France
- Holland
- Germany
- Austria
- Italy
- Bulgaria
- Greece

ASIA
- Israel
- India
- The Philippines
- Thailand

AFRICA
Zambia
South Africa

AUSTRALIA
- Australia

"I was saved at Lakewood Church in 1992. I was a drunken, foul-mouthed woman. I hated God and everything associated with Him. Both John and Dodie prayed for me. Now I'm proud to call Joel and Victoria my pastors."

LINDA NAVEJAR

CHAPTER V

—

Transitional Years

The 90s

Transitional Years

—

In 1990, Lisa Osteen was sorting her father's mail when one of the packages she opened exploded in her lap—it was a mail bomb. Her survival was miraculous, as the mail bomb spewed ten-inch nails that tore holes through the walls of Lisa's office. The Osteen family received an outpouring of support from all over the country, including the president at the time, former President George H. W. Bush. What was expected to be a long recovery only took 6 weeks. That same year, Lisa married Kevin Comes, and the following year Kevin joined the Lakewood staff and is presently the COO of Lakewood.

This same year, Pastor John published his final book, completing his library of thirty-six books with *Seven Qualities of a Man of Faith*. Pastor John's books have been a source of wisdom and encouragement and were translated into many languages for countless individuals around the world.

John and Dodie Osteen receive a get well call from President Bush

Houston Chronicle and Houston Post, January 31, 1990

An Angel in My Office

Lisa Osteen Comes

After removing the last piece of tape from the package in my lap, the next thing I remember is asking God if I was dying. When I came to my senses, I was shaking as if I had been electrocuted and my ears were ringing. Ten-inch nails and shrapnel had ripped holes through my office desk and walls, as well as my right leg and the left side of my abdomen. One of the paramedics on the scene said, "After looking at Lisa's office, someone had to be standing between her and that bomb." We knew it was an angel! It was truly a miracle that I walked away from that scene with no life-threatening injuries.

Houston Chronicle

Vol. 89 No. 110 — Wednesday, Jan. 31, 1990 — 25 Cents

Bomb hurts pastor's daughter

Lakewood Church target of explosive

By ERIC HANSON and JERRY URBAN
Houston Chronicle

Lisa Osteen

The Rev. John Osteen, flanked by his son Joel, left, and Jesse Gallardo, chief of church security, says it was a miracle that his daughter survived a pipe-bomb blast. Lisa Osteen, 31, was opening a package addressed to her father when it exploded Tuesday.

Larry Reese / Chronicle

Lakewood Church members gather outside the church Tuesday morning after a pipe bomb exploded, injuring the pastor's daughter, Lisa Osteen, 31.

Carlos Antonio Rios / Chronicle

Charismatic church a big success story

By JULIA DUIN
Houston Chronicle Religion Writer

Investigators checking past threats on pastor

By JERRY URBAN
Houston Chronicle

Lakewood Church TV production

In the early nineties, Lakewood opened a two-story building that functioned as the Children's Center, serving as the meeting place for over 1,200 kids weekly. The congregation was able to open a three-story Family Life Center that housed church offices, Bible studies, and fellowship groups. Both of these extensions served Lakewood's mission of being a place where people could come to find hope and love.

The next few years were filled with amazing broadcasting opportunities for Lakewood. In 1993, the Super Channel (which broadcasted Pastor John Osteen's messages) was expanded into the Middle East, available with Arabic subtitles. In 1995, Lakewood and the local Christian radio station KSBJ co-produced a youth TV program called "Light Force TV." This program was awarded the CMVS Video Award. During Super Bowl XXXI in 1997, Lakewood locally broadcasted the only Christian commercial. Lakewood produced several one-hour television programs, including a Christmas special and two documentaries, *Death and Beyond* and *Hymns*.

20TH ANNUAL LAKEWOOD CHURCH WORLD CONFERENCE

REACHING THE WORLD FROM HOUSTON

April 21-29, 1990

20th Annual Lakewood Church World Conference

Seven Years of Harvest

Pastor John and Tamara Osteen in India

1990
▸ **January 30:** Lisa Osteen opened a mail bomb that was sent to the church and miraculously survived. She was expected to be out several months in recovery, but returned to work after six weeks and preached.
▸ Pastor John Osteen publishes his final book, *Seven Qualities of a Man of Faith*.

1991
Lakewood Church dedicated a two-story building to be a children's center that allowed for over 1200 children to be ministered to each week.

1993
▸ Lakewood Church opened a three-story family life center, office, and education building.
▸ Super Channel expanded to the Middle East with Arabic subtitles.

1994
▸ **January:** Pastor John Osteen began the "Seven Years of Harvest" to help evangelize the world.
▸ Lakewood Church published a Russian language Bible to be distributed to members of the Russian military.
▸ Lakewood Church launched annual meetings with ministers and pastors who looked to Pastor John as their pastor and mentor.
▸ $40 million of buildings and assets completely paid off.
▸ Lakewood Church became one of the four Houston sponsors for the US Olympics.

Dodie's first pitch at an Astros game

Light Force TV

1995
Lakewood Church and KSBJ's co-produced youth TV program, Light Force TV, was awarded CMVS Video Award.

1997
Lakewood Church locally broadcasted the only Christian commercial during the Super Bowl.

1999
▸ **January 17:** Joel Osteen preached his first message.
▸ **January 23:** Pastor John Osteen went to be with the Lord.
▸ **October:** Joel and Victoria Osteen inaugurated as pastors of Lakewood Church.
▸ Dr. Paul Osteen gave up his successful medical practice to return to Houston and became an associate pastor at Lakewood Church.
▸ Lisa Osteen Comes became an associate pastor at Lakewood Church.
▸ Lakewood Church's TV ministry grew to over 100 countries in over 40 nations.

Pastor John Osteen on missions in India

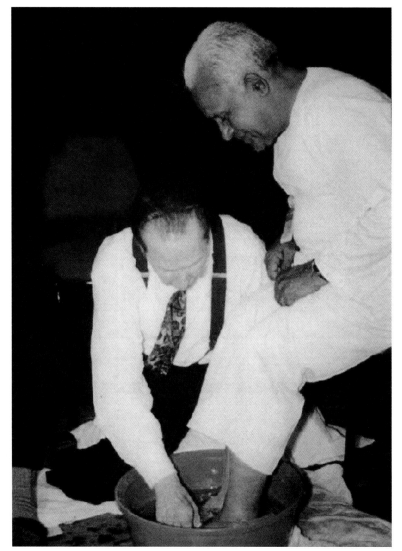

Pastor John Osteen began the "Seven Years of Harvest" to help evangelize the world.

In January 1994, Pastor John began a campaign called "The Seven Years of Harvest" that purposed to fundraise so the Gospel message could be taken further. During this time, Lakewood Church was able to publish a Russian language Bible to be distributed to members of the Russian military—this was a totally miraculous accomplishment. Lakewood regularly held Pastors and Leaders Conferences for pastors and ministers, many of whom launched their ministries through Lakewood Church. Due to the generosity of Lakewood members and its supporters over the years, the church remained debt free and was able to put 40 million dollars toward the building and asset fees of their expansion.

LAKEWOOD CHURCH *presents*

7 *Years of* HARVEST

1994 THROUGH THE YEAR 2000 A.D.

This publication is for our local Lakewood Church members, other local Pastors and their congregations, and television viewers who have invested in our missions thrust to fulfill The Great Commission to go into all the world and preach the Gospel to every creature. Together we are reaching the unreached and telling the untold.

NIGERIAN TELEVISION
Dr. Felix & Esther Okafor

Dr. Felix Okafor and his wife Esther, native Nigerians who attended Lakewood Church for many years, have spearheaded our television outreach in Nigeria. We have been supporting a portion of this outreach for several months, and recently sowed an extra $6,000 into their work.

They are presently airing the "John Osteen" program weekly through three television stations in Nigeria, covering a potential of 45 million souls. Telephone response to the program reveals that both the poor and the rich, top military men and women, politicians, and foreigners working in Nigeria, including Americans, are giving their lives to Jesus or are lifted up as they sit in their living rooms or bedrooms to watch the messages on the nights the program airs.

We also send regular video and audio tapes for their outreach ministries, which has been effective and very instrumental for the healing and restoration of many people. Three state high school boards nominated their ministry to design video projector aided programs to address the issue of arresting the moral decadence, occultism, and disrespect to parents and instituted authorities prevalent in the Nigerian high school student populations. This is a very big task since there are over 600 high schools in these states with a student population of up to half a million students.◆

125 Countries
LAKEWOOD CHURCH
Reaches Via Video
& Audio Tapes
in the English, Spanish, Russian & Bulgarian Languages

ALBANIA	ENGLAND	MALTA	SLOVENIA
ARGENTINA	ESTONIA	MEXICO	SOLOMON
AUSTRALIA	ETHIOPIA	MONACO	ISLANDS
AUSTRIA	FIJI	MONSERRAT	SOUTH
BAHRAIN	ISLANDS	MYANMAR	AFRICA
BARBADOS	FINLAND	NAMIBIA	SOUTH
BELARUS	FRANCE	NEPAL	KOREA
BELGIUM	GERMANY	NETHER-	SPAIN
BELIZE	GHANA	LANDS	SRI
BERMUDA	GIBRALTAR	NEW	LANKA
BHUTAN	GREECE	ZEALAND	SUDAN
BOLIVIA	GUATEMALA	NEW-	SULTANATE
BOSNIA	GUYANA	FOUNDLAND	OF OMAN
BOTSWANA	HAITI	NICARAGUA	SWEDEN
BRAZIL	HONDURAS	NIGERIA	SWITZERLAND
BULGARIA	HONG KONG	NORWAY	TAIWAN
CAMEROON	HUNGARY	PAKISTAN	TANZANIA
CANADA	INDIA	PANAMA	THAILAND
CAYMAN	INDONESIA	PAPUA	TONGA
ISLANDS	IRELAND	NEW GUINEA	TRINIDAD
CHERNAGORA	ISRAEL	PERU	TURK-
CHILI	ITALY	PHILIPPINES	MENISTAN
CHINA	JAMAICA	POLAND	UGANDA
COLUMBIA	JAPAN	PORTUGAL	UKRAINE
COSTA RICA	JORDAN	REP. SOUTH	UNITED ARAB
CROATIA	KAZAHKSTAN	AFRICA	EMIRATES
CUBA	KENYA	ROMANIA	URUGUAY
CYPRUS	KYRGHISTAN	RUSSIA	UNITED
CZECHOSLO-	LATVIA	SAIPAN	STATES
VAKIA	LEBANON	SAUDI	UZBEKISTAN
DENMARK	LIBERIA	ARABIA	VENEZUELA
DOMINICA	LITHUANIA	SCOTLAND	VIETNAM
ECUADOR	MACEDONIA	SERBIA	WEST
EGYPT	MALAWI	SIERRA	INDIES
EL SALVADOR	MALAYSIA	LEONE	ZAIRE
		SINGAPORE	ZAMBIA
			ZIMBABWE

This is my Bible.
I am what it says I am.
I can do what it says I can do.
Today, I will be taught the
Word of God.
I boldly confess: my mind is
alert, my heart is receptive.
I'll never be the same.
I'm about to receive the
incorruptible, indestructible,
ever-living seed of the
Word of God.
I'll never be the same. Never never
never. I'll never be the same.
In Jesus' Name,
Amen.

IN MEMORIUM
John H. Osteen
AUGUST 21, 1921 – JANUARY 23, 1999

Fondly Remembered

Lisa Osteen Comes

When our father passed away, we had no idea of the outpouring of love that we would receive. Not only did the city of Houston extend their support and appreciation, but we received encouragement from all over the world. Our father's life was honored by the national media as well as many newspaper publications.

The memorial service was filled to capacity as friends, congregants, and ministers flew in from all over the United States. My mother was a pillar of strength as she led the memorial service and honored her beloved husband of 44 years. Kenneth Copeland, T. L. Osborn, R. W. Schambach and other notable ministers beautifully honored their longtime friend.

Perhaps the most memorable moment of the service was when my brothers and other family members walked Daddy's casket through the sanctuary of Lakewood Church for the last time as "Amazing Grace" played on the bagpipes. It was his final lap around the sanctuary. Although we were grieving that day, we were all in awe as we saw the amazing effect that one life submitted to the Lord can have on the world.

You Will Know What to Do

Dodie Osteen

When John died, I didn't know what would happen. He had told Lisa more than one time that if anything ever happened to him, we would know what to do, and the Holy Spirit would lead us. I said to the whole congregation, "Please, give me one year to figure out what we're going to do and the kids will speak during the services." And then Joel called me and he said, "Mother, God told me to pastor the church," and I nearly dropped the phone. I said, "Joel, are you sure? You don't know how to preach." He said, "Momma, I'm sure." He got up there the first time, before John's death, and I'm telling you, he was good. The people loved him, but he was shaking. He was so shaky, and he was so young. But I'm telling you, he took it over.

Stepping into the pulpit

Kevin Fujii / Chronicle

Joel Osteen takes over today as pastor of the mega-church founded by his father four decades ago. He went to his mother and siblings a couple of months ago and said he felt called by God to be senior pastor of the 15,000-member Lakewood Church.

Joel Osteen prepared to fill big shoes

By CECILE S. HOLMES
Houston Chronicle Religion Editor

THE REV. JOEL OSTEEN, youngest son of the late John Osteen, becomes senior pastor of Lakewood Church today, moving to the forefront of one of the nation's most successful charismatic ministries after nearly two decades behind the scenes.

Boyish and energetic at age 36, Osteen said in an interview last week that he never intended to be in the pulpit, but he expected to continue assisting his father, one of the city's most recognizable clergymen after years of billboard and TV ad campaigns. For 18 years, Osteen

'This kind of ministry is hard to pass on to another generation. It's been difficult for Billy Graham to pass on to his son (Franklin Graham).'

Lynn Mitchell, resident scholar in religion at the University of Houston

helped edit his father's sermons for television, traveled with him to more than 30 countries and even selected the clothes he wore on camera.

Joel Osteen said he believes that his supporting role helped ready him for leadership of the 15,000-member church.

pastor. The board, which includes family and longtime church members, agreed, though no formal vote was taken.

The selection will be announced to the congregation during services this morning, to warm applause if not to any great surprise, given that Osteen has preached on 33 of the 36 Sundays since his father's death in January.

Yet for the mega-church to thrive under new leadership will be a major accomplishment, a Houston religion scholar said.

"There are not many transitions like this," said Lynn Mitchell, resident scholar in religion at the University of Houston. "This kind of ministry is hard to pass on to an-

"It prepared me greatly," he said. "I was with him every day, day in and day out."

Osteen, who was ordained in January 1992 in a private ceremony by Lakewood's six-member board, went to his family a couple of months ago and told them he believed God wanted him to be senior

See OSTEEN on Page 42A.

A New Assignment

Lisa Osteen Comes

The first time that my brother Joel preached after my father went to heaven, I was sitting behind him in the service like I always did with my father. I leaned forward to remind Joel about an announcement, and as I did, the Lord spoke to me. It was so clear in my spirit. He said, "I am transitioning you to work with your brother. As you served your father, I want you to serve him." I knew at that time that Joel would become the pastor, and I was so excited about my new assignment.

On January 17, 1999, Joel Osteen stepped into the pulpit for the first time. Only 6 days later on January 23, 1999, Pastor John Osteen went to be with the Lord. In October of that year, Joel and Victoria were officially ordained as Lakewood's senior pastors. Dr. Paul Osteen returned to Lakewood to become an associate pastor, giving up a successful medical practice in Little Rock, Arkansas. Lisa Osteen Comes also became an associate pastor after serving for 16 years as the Director of Volunteer Ministries. At this time, Lakewood's TV ministry grew to reach over 100 countries in over 40 nations.

January 17, 1999, Joel Osteen stepped into the pulpit for the first time

Joel Osteen in 1999

"I received Jesus as my Savior in December of 2000. I was 19, severely depressed and did not want to live. I had no hope. I would cry every day, and my poor mom did not know how to help me. As I was scanning through TV, I saw Pastor Joel. I was free; the heavy chains were lifted off me."

ANDREA POTTS-GARDNER

CHAPTER VI

The Compaq Cen

The 00s

Lakewood Church in the year 2000

The Compaq Center

—

In the year 2000, Lakewood saw such growth that they added a third weekend service on Saturday nights. A year later, Lakewood was named by Forbes as the fastest growing and largest nondenominational church in America—God was at work in amazing ways.

Marcos Witt joined the Lakewood pastoral staff in 2002 when Lakewood began its first weekly Spanish service. This service now has several thousand people in weekly attendance.

Joel and Victoria Osteen in front of Compaq Center

Easter at the Ball Field

—

By 2004, Lakewood Church's current location couldn't accommodate the entire congregation. With the Compaq Center renovation unfinished, a new venue was needed. The solution was Houston's Minute Maid Park.

Lakewood Live released its landmark album *We Speak to Nations*. This record sold 100,000 physical copies as Lakewood's sounds of worship traveled around the world. In the following years, the Lakewood Worship Team would release two follow-up albums—*Cover the Earth* and *Free to Worship*. Both of these albums were also hugely successful.

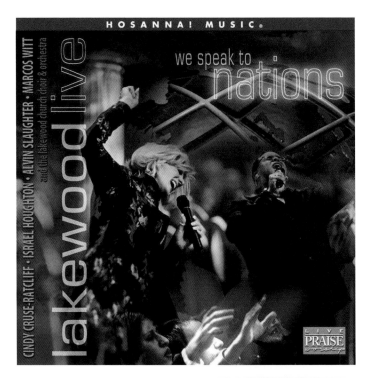

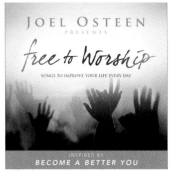

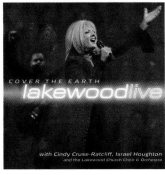

We Speak to Nations; Cover the Earth; Free to Worship

Barbara Walters with Joel and Victoria Osteen;
Marcos Witt joins Lakewood; Cindy Cruse Ratcliff

2000

October: Joel initiated a full Saturday night service in addition to the Wednesday service, two Sunday morning services, and Sunday night service.

2001

‣ Forbes magazine rated Lakewood Church as the fastest growing and largest nondenominational church in America.
‣ Tropical Storm Allison devastated the city of Houston. Lakewood Church houses 3,000 people displaced from the storm and becomes the largest shelter in the city.

2002

‣ **September 15:** Lakewood Church began a weekly Spanish service.
‣ Marcos Witt joined Lakewood Church as pastor of Lakewood Spanish ministries.
‣ Lakewood Live released worship album *We Speak to Nations*.

2004

‣ **January:** Lakewood Church acquired the former Compaq Center.
‣ **October:** *Your Best Life Now* was released and reached #1 on New York Times Bestseller list.
‣ The first Night of Hope took place in Atlanta and was followed by Madison Square Garden.
‣ Victoria hosted the 1st Love Your Life Women's Conference at Lakewood Church.
‣ Lakewood Live released worship album *Cover the Earth*.

2005

July 15: Lakewood Church held its first service in new home at the former and newly renovated Compaq Center.

2006

‣ **December:** Joel Osteen was featured on Barbara Walter's 10 Most Fascinating People list.
‣ The Church Report Magazine named Joel Osteen as the Most Influential Christian in America.

2008

‣ Lakewood Live released worship album *Better Than Life*.
‣ Victoria Osteen published her first book, *Love Your Life*.
‣ Joel and Victoria Osteen published *Hope for Today*, a study Bible.

2009

‣ Lakewood Church launched the Champions Club, a ministry centered on caring for special needs families. Today, there are Champions Clubs on every continent except Antarctica, under the direction of Pastor Craig Johnson.
‣ A Night of Hope: 1st event ever held in the new Yankee Stadium.

Program from Yankee Stadium

Night of Hope Atlanta, 2004; Night of Hope Madison Square Garden, 2004; Joel and Jonathan Osteen at Night of Hope Atlanta

The First "Night of Hope"

Don Jackson

I was in Atlanta in 2004 for the first Night of Hope. No one knew what to expect and it was hard work for everyone. We all had a job to do and we did it. I remember someone saying, "You should see the lines of people outside!" It was amazing. At the end of the night, during the altar call, almost everyone in the building stood up. It was the beginning of great things to come. After fifteen years, it just keeps getting better.

Night of Hope Madison Square Garden, 2004

A Step of Faith

Dr. Paul Osteen

I vividly remember the first Night of Hope in Atlanta in 2004. We had seen such tremendous growth in church attendance at the old location in northeast Houston. It wasn't unusual to have traffic lined up for two miles on the small community roads leading to the church and then for a mile on the main freeway waiting to exit. We had also seen tremendous increase in the TV viewership as well. What we didn't know was whether the people who watched the services on TV would actually come to an event in their city. Renting a huge facility in Atlanta and transporting our whole team to conduct a service was really just a step of faith, "testing the waters" to see if people would attend.

As the time approached for the event to begin, we sent people out to see if there were any people gathering around the entrances, waiting for the event. The reports came back that the only crowds were at a jazz festival being held adjacent to the arena. Our hearts sank, but when the doors opened at 6 p.m., I will never forget it as long as I live. 19,236 people completely filled the room in 20 minutes.

The staff at the arena said they had never seen it fill up so fast. AND, several thousand people watched the service in overflow rooms.

Needless to say, our hearts were overjoyed. I remember walking out with Joel and Victoria and we were overwhelmed at the massive crowd gathered before us. I whispered to Joel, "If you stay humble, there is no telling how God can use you." Later that night during the altar call, conservatively speaking 80 percent of the crowd stood to make Jesus the Lord of their lives. It was an amazing moment.

After 20 years and 197 Night of Hope events, I can personally attest to the fact that Joel continues to be one of the most humble men I know. He hasn't let any of the fame and notoriety and attention change him. He knows that God has given him a unique voice to reach people in our generation. He gives God all the credit and glory. And I am convinced that he will continue to reach people, lift people, give them hope and introduce them to Jesus for many years to come.

Night of Hope New York, 2007; Joel meeting guests after the Night of Hope service;
Sold-out crowd at the Night of Hope, England

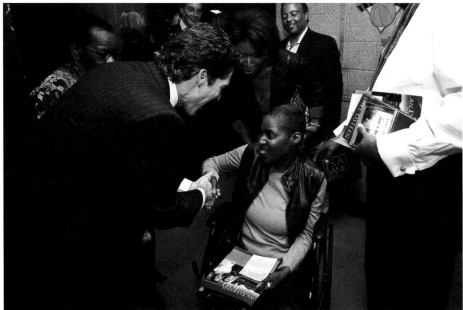

Night of Hope Atlanta, 2004

Groundbreaking Weekend, 2003

A Cold Day

Joel Osteen

In the battle for the Compaq Center, there were a few people that didn't want us to have the building. One of the main business leaders, a very respected, influential man, was at a luncheon with a friend of mine. He said to everyone at the table, "It will be a cold day in hell before Lakewood gets the Compaq Center." He said it very sarcastically, and everyone laughed. Of course, he didn't know my friend was there, and when he told me what the man said, it didn't discourage me, it was just the opposite. It made me more determined. I prayed harder, I stood stronger. Because of God's favor, the former Compaq Center became the home of Lakewood Church. I can imagine now when that businessman drives by the building or he flips through the channel and sees my smiling face, he must think, it's a cold day in hell because here we are.

Houston Mayor Lee Brown presents the key to the Compaq Center

The Groundbreaking Ceremony

Compaq Center
TIMELINE

November
1975

The Summit opened

October 30,
1997

The Summit became the
Compaq Center

Joel and his family add their
inscriptions to the floor

A five-story family life center building is added to the east side of the Compaq Center

Construction being done on the former Compaq Center

Dodie adds her inscriptions, "Great it is to
dream the dream."

Joel on site with Greg Jenkins, architect Jared Wood,
Kevin Comes, and Lisa Ward

2000

Initial Lakewood expansion site fell through

April 6,
2001

The City of Houston announced that they
were seeking proposals to redevelop the
Compaq Center

July 3,
2001

The Houston City Council began
negotiations to lease the Compaq Center to
Lakewood Church

July 5,
2001

Crescent sued to block Houston from leasing
the Compaq Center to Lakewood Church

The interior of the Compaq Center is completely gutted and rebuilt

December 20,
2001

The Houston City Council approved a 60-year lease of the Compaq Center to Lakewood Church

January 2,
2003

Crescent agreed to drop the lawsuit against Lakewood Church to purchase the Compaq Center.

December 1,
2003

Lakewood Church officially assumed control of the Compaq Center

Dec 13-14,
2003

Lakewood Church held groundbreaking weekend services to celebrate

Standing room only at the Grand Opening

The new Lakewood Church

2004

$95 million in renovations began to turn the Compaq Center into the Lakewood Sanctuary

July 16-17, 2005

Over 50,000 people attended the grand opening of the new Lakewood Church

March 31, 2010

In a 13-2 vote, the Houston City Council approved the sale of the former Compaq Center to Lakewood Church. The 7.5 million dollar purchase was approved after initial opposition from several council members

We Got It!

Jonathan Osteen

I still remember exactly where I was when I heard the news. I was 7 years old, watching TV in our living room. My uncle Don burst in, threw his arms in the air, and said, "We got it! We got it!" I didn't really know what we got, but I was excited because he was excited. He told me the city voted and Lakewood now had the Compaq Center, the place where the Rockets won back-to-back championships and some of the most iconic musical artists performed. At the time, I didn't fully understand what that meant. Looking back 16 years later, having seen firsthand the lives changed, I now realize what we got, a building that would be a lighthouse not just for our city, but the world. The Bible says, "One generation will declare Your works to the next and will proclaim Your

A Sunday service at the Lakewood Church

mighty acts." I'm blessed to have had parents and grandparents that stood in faith and dreamed big dreams. I'm honored to serve in the legacy of those who have gone before and continue to dream about all that God still has in store for us. I believe the days ahead of us are greater than the days we leave behind. I am forever grateful that, "We got it."

Victoria Osteen and 2018 speaker Dominique Sachse

2018 speaker Priscilla Shirer; 2017 speaker Lisa Bevere

Love Your Life Women's Event

—

Since 2004, Love Your Life Conference has hosted numerous guest speakers such as Lisa Bevere, Priscilla Shirer, Houston's KPRC Channel 2 evening news anchor Dominique Sachse, It Cosmetic's Jamie Kern Lima, Terri Savelle Foy, and many others.

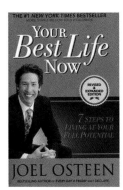
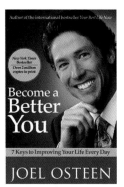

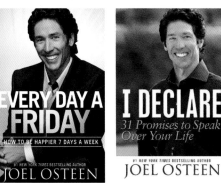
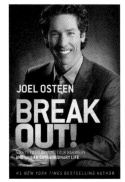
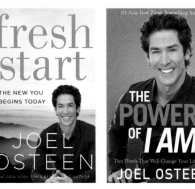
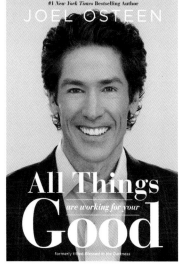

Joel and Victoria Osteen's Books

—

With each book release, Joel takes a tour around the U.S. and is met by long lines of people waiting for the chance to tell him how his books have impacted their personal lives. Much like he does after each weekend service that he preaches, Joel takes the time on those tours to meet and talk with people and sign a copy of his latest book for them.

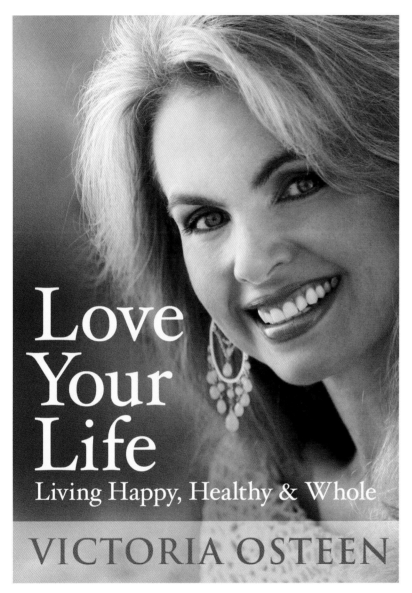

Joel Osteen's book signing event

In January 2004, Lakewood officially acquired the former Compaq Center, the home of the Houston Rockets. Renovation began to transform the basketball arena into a sanctuary.

Joel released his first book, *Your Best Life Now*, in October 2004. It quickly reached #1 on the New York Times Bestseller List, selling more than 1 million copies. At the time of its ten-year anniversary, *Your Best Life Now* had sold over 8 million copies.

In September 2004, Victoria Osteen held the first annual Love Your Life Women's Conference at Lakewood Church.

On July 15, 2005, Lakewood Church held its first service in the former Compaq Center. The 16,000-seat sanctuary was filled to overflowing as people came from all over the country to celebrate the historic event.

With the buzz rising around Lakewood Church and Joel's successful book, Barbara Walters featured Joel as one of her 10 Most Fascinating People in 2006. He was also named by the *Church Report Magazine* as one of the most influential pastors in America.

Victoria Osteen released her first book, *Love Your Life*, in the fall of 2008. Also published this year was Joel and Victoria's *Hope for Today* Study Bible.

Dr. Paul Osteen on mission in Africa, 2007

Africa

Dr. Paul Osteen

When my dad passed away suddenly in January of 1999, we were there with the family during his last hours and there to help with the memorial service. As we drove back to Arkansas after the memorial service, something happened that caught me totally off guard. As we drove past the intersection of US 59 at the exit toward Cleveland, Texas, I heard God speak to me—not in my mind, but deep inside my heart, not audible words, but unmistakable words. He said three phrases, "Give up your practice, move to Houston, and help." Those words made absolutely no sense to my mind but made perfect sense to my spirit. So, at that very intersection, I turned to Jenn and told her what God had spoken. Without hesitation, we both said yes to the new thing God had in store for us.

I thought I was "giving up" my skills as a surgeon. But little did I know, God was working behind the scenes, working to combine those skills in surgery with a clear call to missions—a call He placed on my life when I was a young boy. By listening to His call, it has enabled me to spend several months of the year working in remote parts of Africa helping people who have little to no access to health care or surgery. He has even enabled me to bring my family with me to share in my experiences. It has been nothing short of amazing and the fulfillment of a desire to make a larger impact in the world utilizing my talents as a surgeon and my heart for ministry.

I can say with confidence that our lives are richer, more meaningful and satisfying, than we could have ever imagined. Seeing Joel and Victoria step up, pastor, and lead, seeing what God has done in them and through them, and having the opportunity to be a small part of what God has done here at Lakewood over the past 20 years has been such an honor and privilege. I am so thankful that we obeyed, and I am looking forward to the next 20 years at Lakewood.

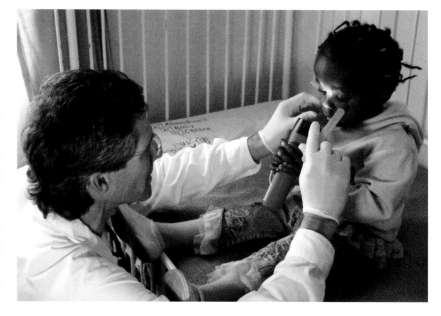

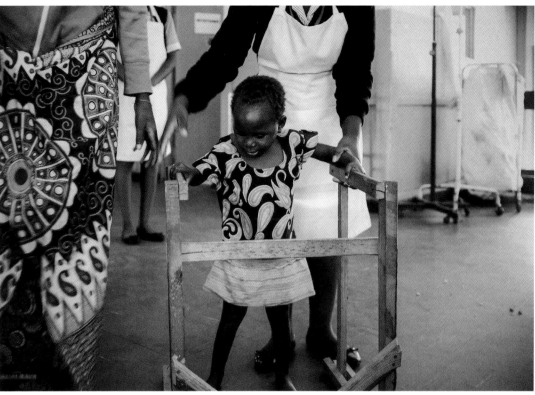
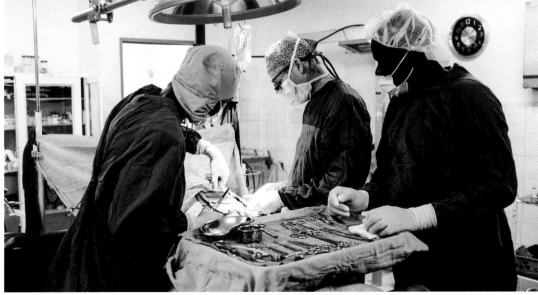

Pastor Craig Johnson's wife, Samantha, and son Connor at the Champions Club Banquet

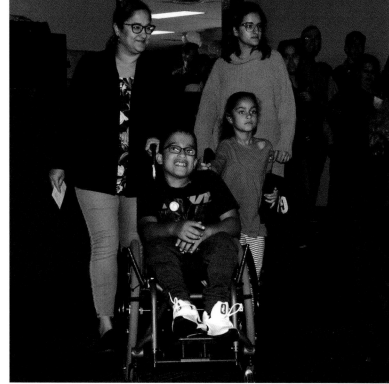

Champions Club doing a special during a weekend service
Pastor Craig Johnson joining his faith with a special needs member

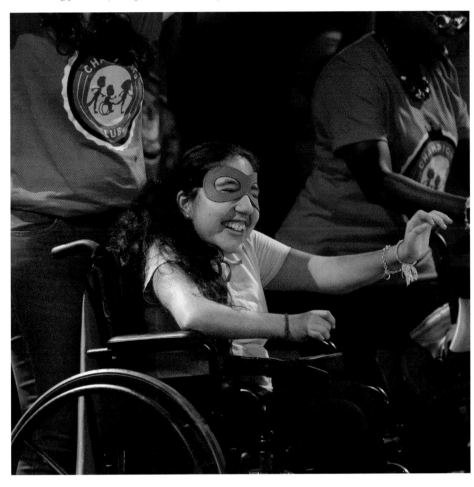

Champions Club

—

Pastor Craig Johnson, one of Lakewood's pastoral staff, launched the Champions Club, a ministry centered on caring for special needs families through providing care for children while their parents attend service as well as emotional support on a personal level. Today, there are Champions Clubs on every continent except Antarctica.

Hurricane Relief

—

HURRICANE
ALLISON RELIEF
2001

HURRICANE
KATRINA–RITA RELIEF
2005

HURRICANE
IKE RELIEF
2008

Certificate presented to Joel Osteen
by the City of Houston after
Tropical Storm Allison, 2002

"*I was going through a difficult time when one Sunday morning I woke up, turned on the TV and saw Joel for the first time. I jumped in my car not knowing why, but drove the 34 miles to Lakewood that morning. It was the beginning of a new life.*"

NATE VAUGHN

CHAPTER VII

Continuing the Legacy

Joel and Victoria Osteen

Victoria Lisa Iloff

—

Victoria Lisa Iloff was raised in Houston, Texas, where her father, Don, was a mathematician with the National Aeronautics and Space Administration (NASA) and her mother, Georgine, founded a successful fine jewelry business.

Along with her brother, Donald, Jr., Victoria grew up in a faithful family regularly attending the Church of Christ where her father served as a deacon and her mother taught Sunday school. After high school, Victoria studied psychology at the University of Houston and worked in her family's jewelry business.

In 1985, she met Joel when he came into her mother's jewelry store to buy a new watch battery. Remarkably, their first date was a Houston Rockets basketball game at the Summit, which was later renamed the Compaq Center. Exactly twenty years after that first date, the building known as the Compaq Center would be renamed again. This time it would be called Lakewood Church.

Joel and Victoria were married in 1987, eighteen months after they first met. Shortly after that she resigned from her family's business and devoted herself to the ministry full time. The change was dramatic and fulfilling. Where she once traveled the magnificent cities of Europe and Asia in search of precious gems, she soon began traveling to the remote and impoverished villages of India and other nations to carry the message of Jesus Christ. Over the next decade, she traveled and ministered with Joel and her father-in-law and supported their efforts to share the Gospel across the globe in every way that she could.

In 1995, she took a break from traveling to give birth to her and Joel's first child, Jonathan. She embraced the role of mother with the same fervor that marked her previous endeavors. Four years later, in 1998, their daughter, Alexandra, was born, and Victoria and Joel's family was complete.

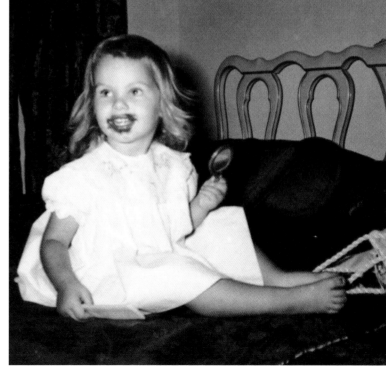

Victoria with her father, Don Iloff;

Victoria as a small child practicing the makeup skills that she would one day use on Pastor John Osteen

Victoria and her brother, Don Iloff Jr.; Victoria as a small girl

Don Iloff, Don Iloff Jr. and Georgine Iloff; Victoria with Joel when they were dating

But 1999 was a bittersweet year. As they celebrated the joy of Alexandra's birth, they found themselves also mourning the loss of Joel's father. As Joel assumed the role of pastor, Victoria's mission was again about to change.

It didn't take long for Victoria to step into her new role. Within the year she began speaking before the congregation and her influence began to grow. She would lead Lakewood's women's ministry and in 2008 wrote her first book, *Love Your Life*. It was an immediate

New York Times bestseller, debuting at #2 on the national bestsellers list.

Victoria's influence has continued to grow. From her popular SiriusXM radio program to her consistently Top 10 podcasts, Victoria continues to encourage and inspire not only the congregation of Lakewood Church, but countless people around the world.

Victoria with Pastor John Osteen

Victoria and Joel; Victoria with Pastor John Osteen riding an elephant in Thailand

Wedding Photo of Joel and Victoria

Joel and Victoria with their children

Victoria on Good Morning America

Joel Scott Osteen

—

Joel Scott Osteen was born in Pasadena, Texas, on March 5, 1963. He is the second youngest of the Osteen children.

Growing up, Joel was always athletic, playing basketball, baseball and running track. After graduation from Humble High School in 1981, he went on to study media at Oral Roberts University, the largest Christian charismatic university in the world.

In 1983, Joel returned to Houston, Texas, to assist his father in developing and overseeing the television ministry at Lakewood Church. For the next 16 years, he produced the John Osteen weekly program as well as many special programs and documentaries. Joel always went the extra mile to make sure the lighting was perfect and camera angles were just right. He would even pick out a suit and tie for his father to wear to make sure he looked his best on camera.

While directing the television ministry, Joel would often assist his father on mission trips around the world, including India, Thailand, and Ecuador. On these trips Joel would travel with a camera to film his father's efforts of sharing the Gospel with the world.

In 1985, Joel met Victoria while purchasing a battery for his watch at her family's jewelry store. The two went on their first date to a Rockets basketball game at the Summit. Twenty years later, the Summit, later called the Compaq Center, would become the home of Lakewood Church.

Joel and Victoria married in 1987. Together they would travel with Joel's father, continuing to aid him in his global outreach. In 1995, they welcomed their first child into the world, Jonathan Osteen. Four years later, in 1998, they would have their second child, Alexandra Osteen.

In January 1999, Joel's father passed away and Joel would follow in his footsteps as the senior pastor of Lakewood Church. People from all over began to visit Lakewood Church and watch the weekly TV broadcast to hear what Joel had to say. They were instantly captivated by his messages of hope, purpose and having a positive outlook. The number of members began to grow and yet again Lakewood would have to find a new and bigger home.

In 2004, Joel and Victoria would secure a lease agreement with the city of Houston to make the former Compaq Center the new home of Lakewood Church.

Continuing the success of the TV outreach, Joel released his first book, *Your Best Life Now: 7 Steps to Living at Your Full Potential*, in October 2004. The book became a #1 New York Times Bestseller and remained on the list for 100 weeks. That same year, Joel launched *Night of Hope* with a 15-city tour that started with sold-out events in Atlanta, Los Angeles, and Madison Square Garden.

The growing popularity of Lakewood Church would bring Joel into interviews with top television personalities such as Larry King, Oprah Winfrey, Jimmy Fallon, and Barbara Walters, who named him as one of the 10 Most Fascinating People of 2006. He would also be able to meet with widely known evangelist, Rev. Billy Graham, and the former president of Israel, Shimon Peres.

Joel, Tamara and their father; Joel in front of childhood home with family dog Rusty

Joel and his father;
Joel's Christmas gifts;
Playing baseball

In June 2009, Forbes magazine named Lakewood Church, under the leadership of Joel, as the largest and fastest growing church in the nation. Carrying his father's vision to reach the world, Joel would bring Lakewood into a new era of media with Lakewood's weekly worship services being broadcast in America's largest TV markets and in more than 100 nations worldwide. Many publications named Joel Osteen the most influential Christian in America and rated Lakewood's broadcast as the top inspiration program on television.

In October 2009, Joel and Victoria held their first *America's Night of Hope*, filling the new Yankee Stadium to capacity. It was a historic occasion as it was the first event to ever be held in the new Yankee Stadium. In subsequent years, Joel and Victoria would fill Dodger Stadium (2010), U.S. Cellular / White Sox Stadium in Chicago (2011), Nationals Park in Washington, D.C. (2012), Marlins Stadium in Miami (2013), Yankee Stadium again (2014), AT&T Park / Giants Stadium in San Francisco (2015), and Comerica Park / Tiger Stadium in Detroit (2016).

In 2014, SiriusXM Radio launched the Joel Osteen Radio Channel 128, a 24-hour channel dedicated to airing Joel's sermon library as well as live broadcasts of Lakewood services, Night of Hope events and weekly call-in shows hosted by Joel and Victoria. The channel quickly became one of SiriusXM's most popular and remains so today.

In 2019, Joel served as the Executive Producer for *Jesus: His Life*, an epic 4-part History Channel series.

To date, Joel has authored over 15 books and devotionals and launched a top-rated podcast. He continues to lead Lakewood Church, release a new book each year, travel to different cities each year on the Night of Hope tours, and host a daily radio program on SiriusXM.

Joel with his dad, Pastor John Osteen; Joel and Victoria

Joel on SiriusXM radio program; Joel Osteen at Dodger Stadium
for a Night of Hope; Joel with his dad, Pastor John Osteen

President George H. W. Bush; Jimmy Fallon;
Rev. Billy Graham; Oprah Winfrey

Joel and Victoria with Larry King; Joel Osteen with Israel Prime Minister Simone Perez;
Joel and Victoria praying over New York City; Joel with Morgan Freeman

"My son was born with a birth defect. After years of disappointment and despair, I cried out to Jesus and was led to Lakewood Church, where my son and I rededicated our lives to Christ. Shortly after, God answered my prayers and my son was healed! Thank God—He is faithful!"

ALIA BENAVIDES

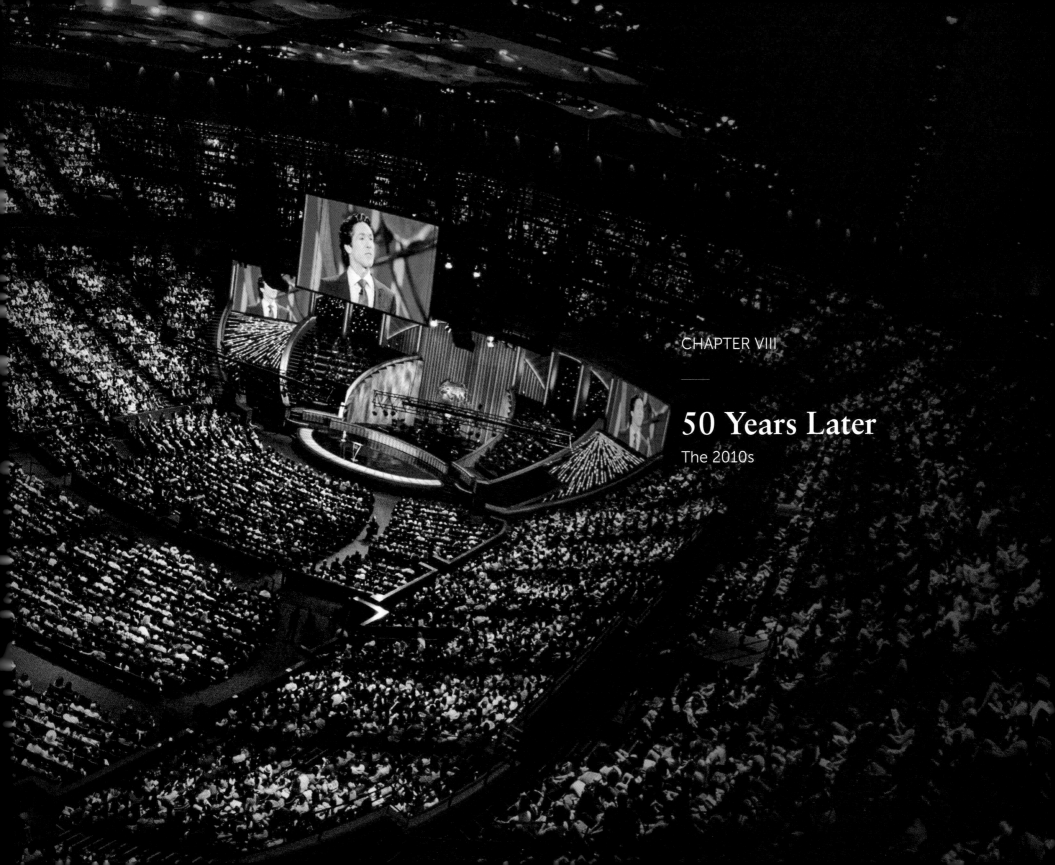

CHAPTER VIII

50 Years Later

The 2010s

50 Years Later

—

Lakewood officially acquires the deed for the Compaq Center as Houston City Council voted 13-2 in favor of Lakewood owning the facility. Lakewood Church and Joel Osteen Ministries win the WEBAWARD for Best Faith-based Website. Dodie Osteen began her prayer and healing drive-up service for those who are unable to walk.

GLAD
Smile
IT'S SUNDAY
LAKEWOOD CHURCH
Hope
IS IN THE HOUSE
LAKEWOOD CHURCH

Joel and Victoria Osteen

Lakewood Church partners with Mark Burnett and Roma Downey for The Bible Miniser

2010
▶ Houston City Council voted 13-2 to sell the former Compaq Center to Lakewood Church and Lakewood Church procured the deed for the facility.
▶ Lakewood Church and Joel Osteen Ministries won WEBAWARD for Best Faith-based Website.
▶ Dodie Osteen began drive-thru healing service at Lakewood Church.

2012
Lisa Osteen Comes published *You Are Made for More! How to Become All You Were Created to Be.*

2014
Joel Osteen began hosting Joel Osteen Radio on SiriusXM 128.

2016
▶ Dodie Osteen published *If My Heart Could Talk: A Story of Family, Faith, and Miracles.*
▶ Dr. Paul Osteen hosted the 1st annual M3 Missions Conference at Lakewood Church.
▶ Lakewood Church hosted the 1st annual Spark: A Marriage Conference with Lakewood's Marriage and Family Pastors, Clayton and Ashlee Hurst.

Harvey Relief Concert

Pastors Danilo and Gloriana Montero

Alexandra Osteen sings with Lakewood Worship

2017
October 13: Lakewood Church teamed up with KSBJ to host the Houston Worship Relief Concert.

2018
▸ **August 14:** Mayor Sylvester Turner honored the Osteen family and Lakewood Church by declaring August 14 as "Lakewood Church Day."
▸ **September 14:** Lakewood Music released its first worship album in ten years, *Live in the Wonderful*.
▸ **September 23:** Jonathan Osteen preached his first sermon at the Sunday night Lakewood Young Adults service.

In 2016, Dodie Osteen published the story of her life in *If My Heart Could Talk: A Story of Family, Faith and Miracles*.

Joel and Victoria Osteen on SiriusXM

SiriusXM approached Joel with the opportunity to have a channel that would continually broadcast the Lakewood services live as well as his messages. Countless stories of lives changed have poured in since the SiriusXM Channel 128 was launched.

Joel and Victoria Osteen with pastors from the Champions Network

Pastor Phil Munsey

CHAMPIONS
Network

The Champions Network

—

Created by Joel in 2010 with the help of
Pastor Phil Munsey, the Champions Network
is designed to connect new believers that
watch our broadcasts with good, Bible-based
churches in their area. Now numbering over
570 churches, these ministries continue to
transform lives across the country.

Joel Osteen speaks at Yankee Stadium

America's Night of Hope

—

Starting with 2009's historic Night of Hope at Yankee Stadium, the America's
Night of Hope events bring Joel's message of hope to packed stadiums
across the country. These major events are broadcast live nationally on
partners such as TBN and have reached hundreds of thousands
of people in major U.S. cities.

AMERICA'S NIGHT OF HOPE EVENTS

April 25, 2009 Yankee Stadium New York, NY	August 6, 2011 U.S. Cellular Field Chicago, IL	April 20, 2013 Marlins Park Miami, FL	August 8, 2015 AT&T Park San Francisco, CA
April 24, 2010 Dodger Stadium Los Angeles, CA	April 29, 2012 Nationals Park Washington, DC	June 7, 2014 Yankee Stadium New York, NY	July 23, 2016 Comerica Park Detroit, MI

First event and celebration of faith in the new Yankee Stadium, 2009

A truly historic moment took place in 2009 when Lakewood held America's Night of Hope in the new Yankee Stadium. This event was the first event held in the stadium only nine days after it had opened. Approximately 50,000 people gathered that day to hear the message of hope in Christ.

America's Night of Hope

Dodie Osteen sharing her testimony of healing at America's Night of Hope;
A crowd of approximately 50,000 people at America's Night of Hope at the new Yankee Stadium, 2009

Victoria and Alexandra visiting students of a local elementary in Washington, D.C.; Jonathan and Young Adult Pastor Nick Nilson serving at a local elementary school

Generation Hope Project®

—

Launched as part of the 2012 America's Night of Hope in Washington, D.C., Generation Hope Project® brought together hundreds of volunteers from around the world to share hope with communities in need. Led by Jackelyn Viera Iloff, volunteers worked with dozens of local community organizations, donated thousands of volunteer hours, and blessed countless families and individuals in the major metropolitan areas visited by America's Night of Hope.

Jackelyn Viera Iloff (right) and Dodie Osteen with a volunteer during a Generation Hope Project® community outreach.

Jonathan Osteen; Pastor John Gray;
Young Adult Pastors Nick and Summer Nilson in 2012

Hope & Life Conference

—

In the summer of 2011, Lakewood Church held the first annual Hope and
Life Youth and Young Adult Conference under the leadership of Young
Adult Pastors Nick and Summer Nilson. Hope and Life continues to gather
thousands from all over the world. This three-day conference is hosted free
of charge so that anyone can come to lift up the Name of Jesus and
be encouraged by amazing speakers.

Hope and Life Conference

Over 100 vendors set up throughout the lobby

Dr. Paul Osteen speaking at 2017 M3 Conference

M3 Conference

—

Dr. Paul organized and hosted the first annual M3 Medical Missions Conference at Lakewood Church, with hundreds of medical professionals and missionaries in attendance from across the world.

Dr. Paul and his family; 2017 keynote speaker Bob Goff; The Samaritan's Purse Mobile Field Hospital exhibit

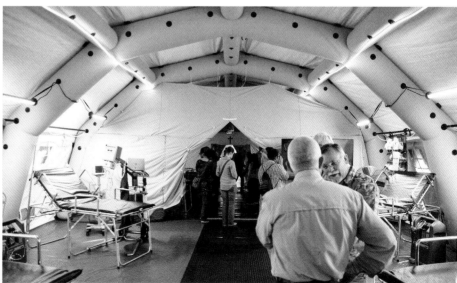

Pastor Nick Nilson hosts panel with Joel and Victoria at the annual Spark marriage conference

Dr. Gary Chapman; Pastors Clayton and Ashlee Hurst; Pastor Nick Nilson with Pastors Robert and Taylor Madu

Spark: A Marriage Conference

—

In the fall of 2016, Lakewood hosted its the first annual marriage conference, *Spark*, under the leadership of our Marriage Ministry pastors, Clayton and Ashlee Hurst. This conference and ministry continues to impact many marriages and individual lives.

Pastors Danilo and Gloriana Montero

Spanish Lakewood Music album and single

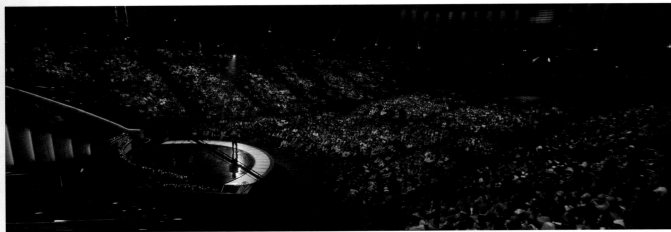

Iglesia Lakewood

—

In 2002, Lakewood Church added a Spanish service to the weekend services. Since then, this service has grown to have thousands in weekly attendance. In 2012, Danilo and Gloriana Montero became the head pastors of the Spanish congregation.

For the past 17 years, the Spanish ministry team has hosted health fairs, begun services for youth and young adults, and launched Grupos con Vida to connect with the city's large demographic of Spanish-speaking people of all ages.

In 2016, Iglesia Lakewood held its first annual 3-day conference, Festival Lakewood, which has over 3,000 in attendance from all over the world. In 2019, the Spanish worship team released their first album, *En Tus Maravillas*. The single from this album, *Me Rodeas*, sung by worship leader Ingrid Rosario, charted #1 on Miami radio.

In September 2017, the city of Houston was devastated as Hurricane Harvey tore through the city. Lakewood Church was able to act as a shelter and donation center for hundreds of families and individuals. To aid with fundraising for recovery efforts, Lakewood partnered with KSBJ, hosting the Houston Worship Relief Concert that featured Hillsong Worship, Elevation Worship, Kari Jobe, Bethel Music, and many others.

The following year, Mayor Sylvester Turner honored Lakewood Church for all of the recovery work accomplished after Hurricane Harvey, naming August 14 as "Lakewood Church Day" in the city of Houston.

Hurricane Harvey

LAKEWOOD RESPONDS

—

OVER

9,300

VOLUNTEERS
MOBILIZED

OVER

1,000

HOME CLEAN OUTS

40

HOMES ENTIRELY
REBUILT

Lakewood hosts Congregation Beth Yeshurun for their services after Harvey

Lakewood hosts the Houston Worship Relief Concert, featuring Kari Jobe, Hillsong Worship and more.

**DIRECT FINANCIAL
ASSISTANCE TO OVER**

2,100

HOUSTON-AREA FAMILIES

ESTIMATED

296,592

**WATER BOTTLES
DISTRIBUTED**

ESTIMATED

70,000

**HOURS CONTRIBUTED
BY VOLUNTEERS**

Newly renovated home being presented with Pastor Craig Johnson

Lakewood Music album and Young Adult single

Lakewood Music

—

In September 2018, Lakewood Church released its first album in 10 years titled, *Live in the Wonderful*. The following year, in April 2019, the Spanish version, *En Tus Maravillas*, was released. This album is a very honest attempt to capture what an average weekend at Lakewood sounds like. Live in the Wonderful is the sound of one Church with many harmonies in one Voice.

Lakewood Music continues to work on music, with a young adult EP, *In the Name*, scheduled to release in the summer of 2019.

Lakewood Music team

Jonathan Osteen

—

At a young age, Jonathan began traveling with the ministry on both Night of Hope events and mission trips. Soon after, he committed to serving as part of the worship team where he continues to lead today.

He graduated from the University of Texas at Austin in 2017 with a degree in Radio, Television, and Film. He now works in the music and creative departments of the church with a passion for reaching every generation in unique and meaningful ways. He enjoys songwriting, storytelling, and values God's heart for people above all else.

Jonathan with his grandfather, Pastor John Osteen; Jonathan with a family pet

Jonathan Osteen as a young boy; Jonathan with his father, Joel Osteen

Jonathan on stage with his father, Joel Osteen, at Easter 2004; Jonathan playing guitar during an Easter service at Lakewood Church; Jonathan on a mission trip

Jonathan leading worship during a weekend service at Lakewood Church

Alexandra Osteen

—

At the age of 5, Alexandra began singing the closing song at the Night of Hope events. With a sincere and gentle voice, she has continued to lead worship in many areas of the church throughout the years. She has served alongside her parents on community outreaches, mission trips, and has a heart to help people.

In 2016, Alexandra began attending the University of Texas at Austin where she studies communications. She is dedicated to honoring God, building His house, and spreading the message of hope.

Alexandra as a baby with her mother, Victoria Osteen; Alexandra with her brother, Jonathan Osteen

Alexandra singing during a Night of Hope

Alexandra with her father, Joel Osteen, at a Night of Hope; Alexandra fishing with her father;
Alexandra with a family pet; Alexandra with her mother on a mission trip

Alexandra leading worship during a weekend service at Lakewood Church

Monday Night Bible Study

—

In 2017, Lakewood Church began hosting a weekly Bible study on Monday nights. Through teachings from Dr. Paul Osteen and Pastor Lisa Osteen Comes, along with Pastor Erik Luchetta and Youth Director Jeremy Marrone, thousands of people, in person and online, receive lessons on topics such as prayer, miracles, and Christian living through Scripture.

Prayer and Healing Service

—

Since 1981, Dodie Osteen has been a faithful advocate of prayer and miracles because of the miraculous healings she has experienced in her own life. For decades, she has hosted prayer and healing services where people from all walks of life can receive prayer for healing in their bodies. In recent years, Dodie added a drive-up healing service to make accessibility easier for those in need of prayer and a healing service specifically for children with special needs and their families.

Dodie stands on the belief that if "God did it for me, He can do it for you!" She continues to pray over every seat in the main sanctuary at Lakewood Church, for every person who visits, and around the 610 Loop over the entire city of Houston.

Water Baptism

—

Starting in 2017, Lakewood Church began hosting church-wide mass baptisms with people traveling from all over the world to be baptized personally by Joel Osteen. For the past three years, over 4,000 people have been baptized. The church continues to hold mass baptisms with the hope of changing the lives of many more!

OVER

4,000

BAPTIZED

OVER

880,000

FACEBOOK LIVE VIEWS

Joel Osteen doing church-wide water baptism.

The Heart of a Servant

—

From the original 90 members to the thousands of faithful volunteers, Lakewood Church thrives because of the willingness of every member and volunteer to serve alongside the Osteen family. Each week, longtime members and volunteers can be seen serving in all capacities from childcare to greeting, from ushering to singing in the choir, and from operating cameras to being prayer partners. It is because of all of you that Lakewood Church is able to celebrate 60 years. Thank you!

Victoria Osteen speaking during a weekend service at Lakewood Church

Victoria Osteen meeting the young members of Lakewood Church; Dodie Osteen riding a golf cart through the church, greeting members

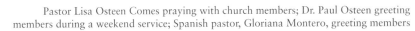

Pastor Lisa Osteen Comes praying with church members; Dr. Paul Osteen greeting members during a weekend service; Spanish pastor, Gloriana Montero, greeting members

Joel Osteen onstage during a weekend service at Lakewood Church;
Pastor John Gray at Lakewood Church

Victoria Osteen praying for a member during service;
Victoria's brother, Don Iloff, speaking at a Night of Hope

Lakewood Church worship leaders, Peter Wilson, Steve Crawford, and Cindy Cruse Ratcliff

Joel Osteen behind the scenes

Joel Osteen checking cameras; Joel and Victoria during a video shoot;
Joel Osteen doing a production run through for a Night of Hope

Life Groups

KidsLife

Block Parties

Wednesday Night Service

Pastor Nick Nilson; Pastor Lisa Osteen Comes; Pastor John Gray;
Dr. Paul Osteen; Pastor Craig Johnson

Spanish High School Pastor Abner España praying with students; Youth Summer Camp 2017;
Lakewood Youth service; Youth Director Jeremy Marrone; Youth Summer Camp 2016

Lakewood Youth

Members of Lakewood Youth in Haiti; Lakewood Missions team in India;
Pastor Ashlee Hurst in Guatemala; Lakewood Men's Ministry on site in Belize

Lakewood Missions

Joel and Victoria Osteen with Pastor Craig Johnson at the opening of a new Champions Club location; Lakewood Missions team at the Houston Food Bank

Lakewood Missions team serving meals to the homeless; Lakewood Missions Servolution "Angel Tree"

Joel with Lakewood Staff praying over the seats in the Sanctuary

This book, Legacy of Hope, is special to Victoria and me because of what it represents — that when you stay faithful to what God has called you to do, you can accomplish more than you ever dreamed possible. For 60 years, the family of Lakewood believers have worked faithfully and tirelessly together with the Osteen family to share the love, hope, and salvation of Jesus throughout the world. You are a member of this family and we are grateful for the prayers, support, dedication, and faithfulness you have shown throughout all of these years. Through every change, expansion, and new territory the church has experienced, it was you, the faithful members of Lakewood Church, who stood with us in our pursuit to reach the unreachable, touch the untouchable, and love the unlovable through the message of HOPE in Jesus Christ.

We are here today because we stand on the shoulders of those who came before us. It was the faithfulness of a young minister, his wife, and 90 dedicated believers that a small neighborhood church grew into one of the largest and most influencial churches in the world. From those humble beginnings, Lakewood Church has experienced the unprecedented favor of God in the most miraculous and undeniable ways, and today, in this generation, He continues to show us His favor and to crown our efforts with success.

It is our purpose to share with you this look at the history of Lakewood Church so that you too can appreciate and enjoy the remarkable journey of our church and those who made it possible. When we take the time to remember and appreciate all of the good things God has done for us, it allows us to look to the future with expectation and excitement.

IF He has done it FOR us in the past, He will surely do it FOR us in the FUTURE. Enjoy this book, celebrate the great things God has done FOR us, and know that while our past has been Filled with victory, blessings and miracles, our best days are yet to come!
We love and appreciate you very much!

Joel + Victoria Osteen

Ah, great it is to believe the dream
as we stand in youth by the starry stream;
but a greater thing is to fight life through
and say at the end, the dream is true!

JOHN OSTEEN
orig. Edwin Markham